Horses&Homes

Horses&Homes

written and photographed by Jenifer Jordan

GIBBS SMITH
TO ENRICH AND INSPIRE HUMANKIND
Salt Lake City | Charleston | Santa Fe | Santa Barbara

First Edition
13 12 11 10 09   5 4 3 2 1

Published by
Gibbs Smith
P.O. Box 667
Layton, Utah 84041

Orders: 1.800.835.4993
www.gibbs-smith.com

Designed by Debra McQuiston
Printed and bound in China
Gibbs Smith books are printed on either recycled, 100% post-consumer waste, FSC-certified papers or on
paper produced from a 100% certified sustainable forest/controlled wood source.

Library of Congress Cataloging-in-Publication Data

Jordan, Jenifer.
  Horses and homes / written and photographed by Jenifer Jordan. — 1st ed.
      p. cm.
  ISBN-13: 978-1-4236-0509-6
  ISBN-10: 1-4236-0509-8
  1. Collectibles in interior decoration. 2. Horses—Collectibles. 3. Horsemanship—Miscellanea. I. Title.
  NK2115.5.C58J67 2009
  747—dc22
                          2008054130

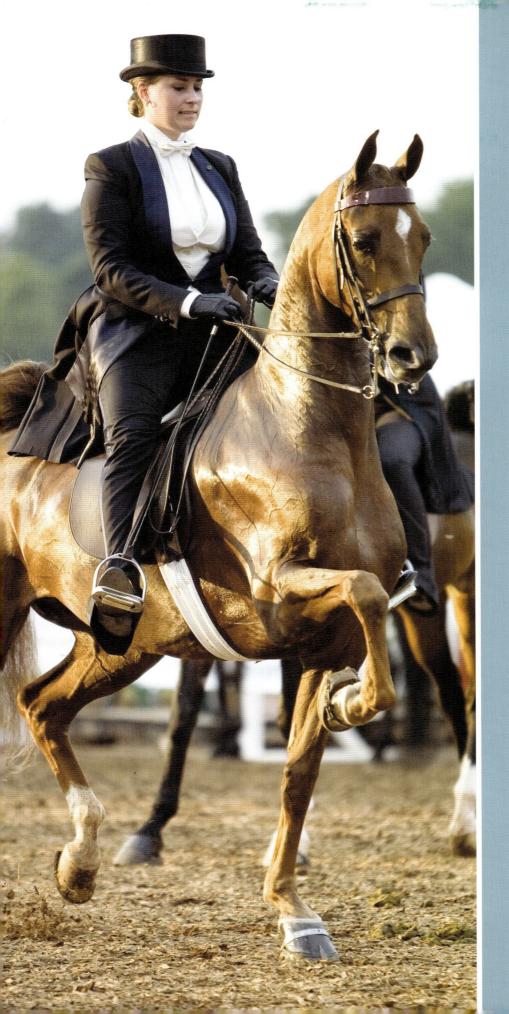

To my father, Harry,
who shared with me his
love of horses.

CONTENTS

FOREWORD

When I first met Jenifer Jordan almost twenty years ago, she was photographing my home for a national magazine. She was at ease behind the camera, went about her business in a very professional manner, and produced beautiful photographs. I was sold on her talent immediately.

Many photo shoots and several homes later, we discussed collaborating on a book. We each thought we had one book in us. Three books later and after travels to Spain, Jamaica, Washington, D.C., Virginia, and all over Oklahoma, Texas, and Florida, we have no secrets. We have had a wonderful journey together, and I am honored to count Jenifer as a very special and dear friend.

This book, *Horses & Homes*, is truly a passion project for Jenifer because it sprang from her own lifestyle. Her love and understanding of all things equine is revealed in every photograph. And to me that is the mark of a true animal lover and a very gifted photographer, author, and stylist. Thank you, Jenifer, for an inspiring and beautiful book!

—Charles Faudree

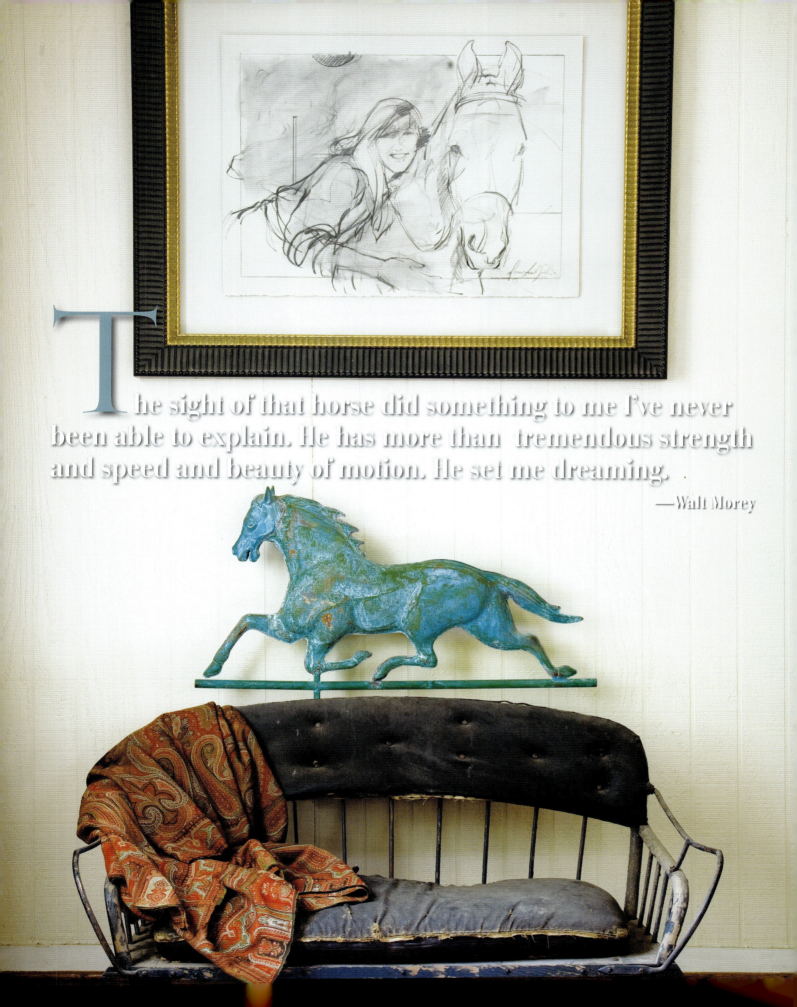

The sight of that horse did something to me I've never been able to explain. He has more than tremendous strength and speed and beauty of motion. He set me dreaming.

—Walt Morey

INTRODUCTION

The love of a horse shows no boundaries—not only for riders but also for anyone who can appreciate nature's true beauty. To me a horse means not just unconditional love and friendship, but a calm and peace in life—like coming home.

In my research of what to include in this book, I found an abundance of homes with an equine influence. I also found these home owners to be very generous with their homes and horses, and very helpful in introducing me to their friends whose love of horses also proved evident in their design choices. It is apparent in the homes I photographed for this book that there is a common love of horses. Though each home was different, I loved the flow and the connection that they brought to my book.

In the homes that appear in this book, the horse is an integral design element in many ways, from oil paintings and bronze sculptures to country French toile fabrics and weather vanes. The use of horses in various décor represents different things

to these home owners. The art of horses represented love in one home, pure strength, true beauty moving through life, the unconditional love, a calm and peace, and also freedom. In another home the horses brought back childhood memories, and in another the décor represents "making it" and being able to live in the country. Whatever the representation, I hope *Horses & Homes* captures the hearts of horse lovers and non-horse lovers alike so that everyone sees nature's true beauty through the horse and the calm and freedom horses represent.

My love of horses came from my father, Harry. When I was eleven he bought me my first horse, an albino half-Arabian half-Morgan named Prince. Pure white with baby-blue eyes, Prince had the most beautiful long blond mane and tail, which I was very jealous of as a little girl. I think it was then that I found the passion for horses that would last me a lifetime. Prince was my best friend, and I used to find myself lost in moments with him, spending my days—and nights, if I had anything to do with it—with him. We could ride for hours. A favorite path took us to a nearby creek to go swimming, before everything was fenced off in the Texas countryside. I would find a green pasture for him to enjoy, take off his bridle, lay with him in the grass, and relax and enjoy the peace and solace of the country. Sometimes I would camp out in his stall with him, and I often found myself in trouble with my parents for not making it home in time for dinner—back when dinners were spent together as a family. Thanks, Mom. It was truly a simpler time in my life when I first experienced the respect, the friendship, and the unconditional love of a horse.

Then life sort of happened. I got out of horses for a while, but I never lost my passion for them. In my twenties and thirties, I was obsessed with my career until one day I thought, "I work too hard. I need to enjoy life more." I quickly remembered my childhood memories and the fun times I had with my dear friend, Prince. It did not take long for me to make my decision at age thirty-eight to buy a horse—my first American Saddlebred. Johnny G would fast become a special part of my life, and I once again experienced that unconditional love of a horse that I had with Prince. Getting horses back into my life gave me something. It gave me back living in the moment; it gave me back a peace of mind and an appreciation of life. It helped me escape the rat race. It brought me back home. It actually made me a better me; it certainly made me a better photographer! Thank you, Johnny G.

My Saddlebred experience then led me to my five-gaited friend, Jack, whose show name is My Secret Passion. I think I can safely say that our passion was to "rack on!" Jack and I shared a connection, and we both had a definite need for speed! Being in the show ring with Jack was a fun and exciting time, and we won many blues and championships together. Thanks, Jack!

Having horses in my life gave me a reason to work harder—so I could play harder. Because of this, in my twenty-five-year career as an interior and architectural photographer, I am honored to include hundreds of design magazines and design books in my portfolio, and I'm still going strong. *Horses & Homes* will be the sixth book that I've exclusively photographed, and the first that I have been lucky enough to write.

—Jenifer Jordan

Here we are! My Secret Passion (Jack), my five-gaited Saddlebred, and me in the show ring. Photo by Todd Macklin.

HUNTING

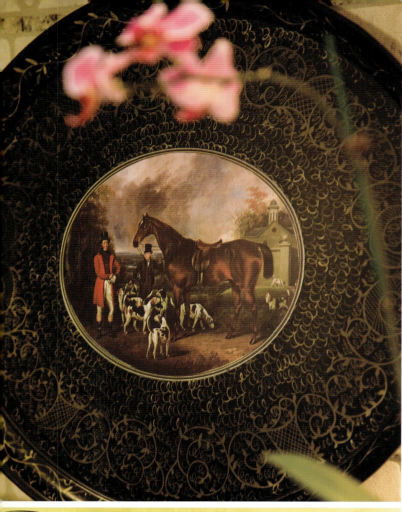

Lynn's bedside table elegantly displays her hunter background. An iron hitching-post top has been repurposed as a lamp, and competition photos are proudly displayed, *previous overleaf.*

The

hunting horse is a type of horse, not a breed. Hunting is a discipline, a traditional sport that began in Britain and Ireland over three thousand years ago as the pursuit of a wild animal in its own environment by men on horses and their hounds. These horsemen hunted fox, stag, boar, and fallow deer, to name a few. These horses, also known as hunters, were bred for their stamina and fitness to last for hours in keeping up with the hounds at an even pace until the animal was captured. Hunters also had to be able to jump a variety of obstacles like stone fences and dykes. The sport certainly began in the field, though it is impossible to look at hunters isolated only in the field. Today the hunters are not only hunting foxes with their hounds, but they are now competing in show jumping, the show ring, the steeplechase, and horse trials.

Look, what a horse should have he did not lack, save a proud rider on his back.

—Shakespeare

In the show ring there are two divisions:

hunters and jumpers. A hunter is judged on how he moves, his conformation, and his performance. A hunter needs to have an even pace, a speed that would simulate keeping up with the hounds and other horses in a fox hunt. Hunters in competition also jump; their jumps or fences usually resemble the obstacles that would be in the field (for example, stone fences, posts, rails, brush, or dykes). These jumps or fences average three to four feet in height. The hunter should have a smooth, consistent style over the jumps. A hunter is not judged on speed but on a clean jump, which means no faults against him. A fault is received by knocking over a jump, hitting a jump, or refusing to jump.

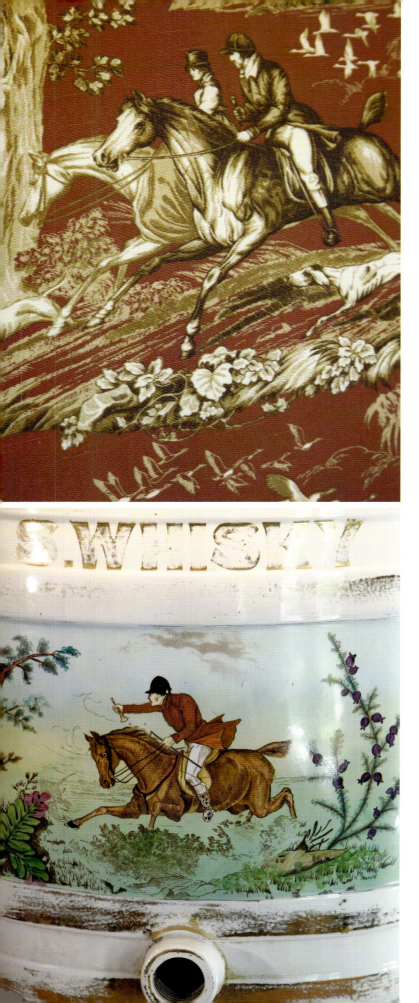

A **Ralph** Lauren fabric of horses, hounds, and riders is deep green and burgundy.

The jumper division, or show

jumping, is judged on speed, the height of the jump, and the cleanness of the jump. The jumpers are not judged on style but on performance. The competition is how fast and how high the horse and rider make it through their ride. Jumper fences typically average four to five feet in height. This division is one of the most popular among spectators. Steeplechasing is a race over jumps. It is horse racing but with jumps on a track, more like hurdles in a track meet. The steeplechaser is also judged on speed and cleanness of the jump. Horse trials are usually a three-day event. This sport began as training for the military. Soldiers needed to be fit to cover long distances and travel over open country, jumping whatever obstacles stood in their paths. In this event, both horse and rider need to be in great shape, have steady nerves, and be confident in each other. Another dance between horse and rider!

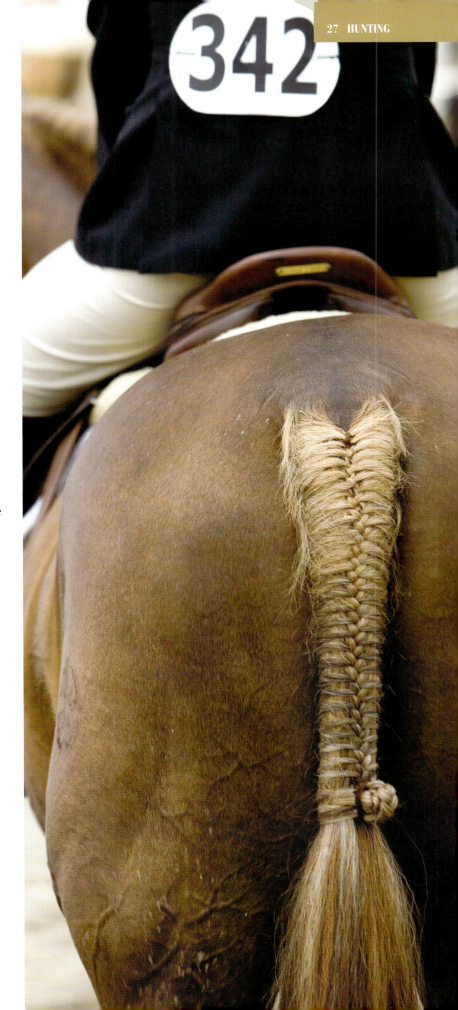

Hunters
—one of the great British traditions—
have become very popular in Europe as well as
in America. The hunter division has now become
the biggest equestrian activity of all time.

MANY DIFFERENT BREEDS OF HORSES AND PONIES ARE USED AS HUNTERS.

My friend Lynn Walsh says
that in addition to Thoroughbreds,
many hunters or jumpers in the United States
are European warmbloods: Hanoverian,
Dutch, Swedish, or Oldenburgs.

A drawing

by Melissa Kahout is a commanding presence above the mantel in Susan Pelletier's great room. Atop the table sits a sculpture by Susan of one of her horses.

The design in

Lynn's home is classic, mixing traditional antiques with a lifetime's worth of competition awards and equine collections and memorabilia. Her home is a showcase of her love of hunters and of the sport. It seems fitting that she should live in an equestrian community.

One of Lynn's neighbors is Susan Pelletier, and they frequently ride together along the lakes and wooded trails. In Susan's classic Texas Hill Country–style great room, she has created an airy and inviting space. The room is a study of old and new, with salvaged antique columns and wonderfully comfy furnishings. In keeping with this style, the room boasts a rustic Texas limestone fireplace with a touch of refinement from a stylish cast-stone mantel instead of the usual rustic wood. Susan's love of horses, and especially hunters, is reflected in subtle equine touches. A drawing by Melissa Kahout rests on the mantel, while a piece of handmade sculpture, Susan's own work, sits on the coffee table and, though small, makes a dramatic impact against the grounding backdrop of the limestone fireplace.

It's quite evident that Susan has a great design sense that can be an inspiration for those hoping to add this look to their home. Texture is an important design element in this room, which Susan has achieved with a mix of limestone, antique wood, stone coffee table, and botanical print chairs.

SHOW JUMPING

This team successfully jumps a fence at the Germantown Charity Horse Show in Tennessee, *right*.

Of all the horse disciplines, show

jumping both impresses and intimidates me. I love watching it, but I don't think I will be trying this event. Forty years ago, I attempted a little jump with Prince. We approached it and he said "no." He went right and I went straight, and I landed headfirst on the bars. Prince came around and looked down at me, nudging me, laughing at me—although truthfully I think my boy came around to help me up!

Horses lend us the wings we lack. —Anonymous

In Bill Mullen's English Country–style warming room, brilliant morning light streams through the large windows. Right off the kitchen, this inviting room is filled with the most exquisite equine treasures. The combination of Bill's antique Windsor chairs with lovely paisley cushions, needlepoint pillows, and antique dog portraits evoke a true English country house. Though located in Oklahoma, one could imagine this comfortable warming room in the Cotswolds of the English countryside—or possibly in a little stone cottage with a thatched roof. Like in those homes, the importance of man's relationship with his horses and dogs is proudly on display.

The focal point of the room, a gorgeous antique wall shelf, showcases Bill's striking collection of horse accoutrements, including his loving cups, Staffordshire bookends, and his riding hat. Predictability in design is never a good thing, and Bill is certainly not predictable—instead of standard matching lamps, he made two custom lamps for this space. One is an antique silver loving cup and the other a timeless Staffordshire figurine, creating a fun and unexpected design statement. Plush chairs and a comfortable sofa make this the ideal space for morning coffee and the newspaper.

A collection of custom riding boots from a vendor's booth at the horse show in Lexington, Kentucky.

Found at the Kentucky Horse Park in Lexington, this pile of brightly colored fence poles is used to create the heights for various competitive jumps.

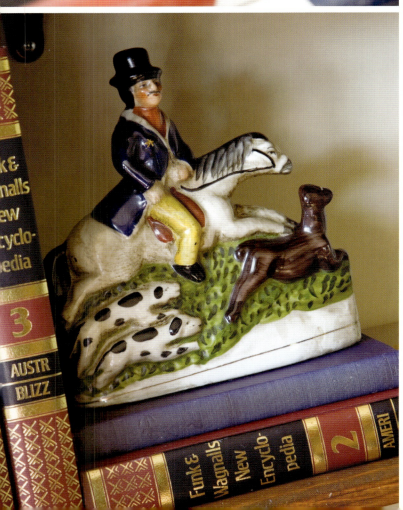

It was in 1788 that jumping was first mentioned in French cavalry manuals, and soon thereafter the British fox hunters wrote of jumping the hedges and fences in the field. In 1865, almost one hundred years later, jumping was officially recorded in Ireland at the Royal Dublin Society's annual show. Then in 1883 at the National Horse Show at Madison Square Garden in New York, jumping was first introduced in the United States. The first show jumping event in the Olympics was in the 1912 games at Stockholm. A good score on a jumping course is based on both a good time and a clean run. It is true beauty in motion to see a team of horse and rider gracefully scale the fences.

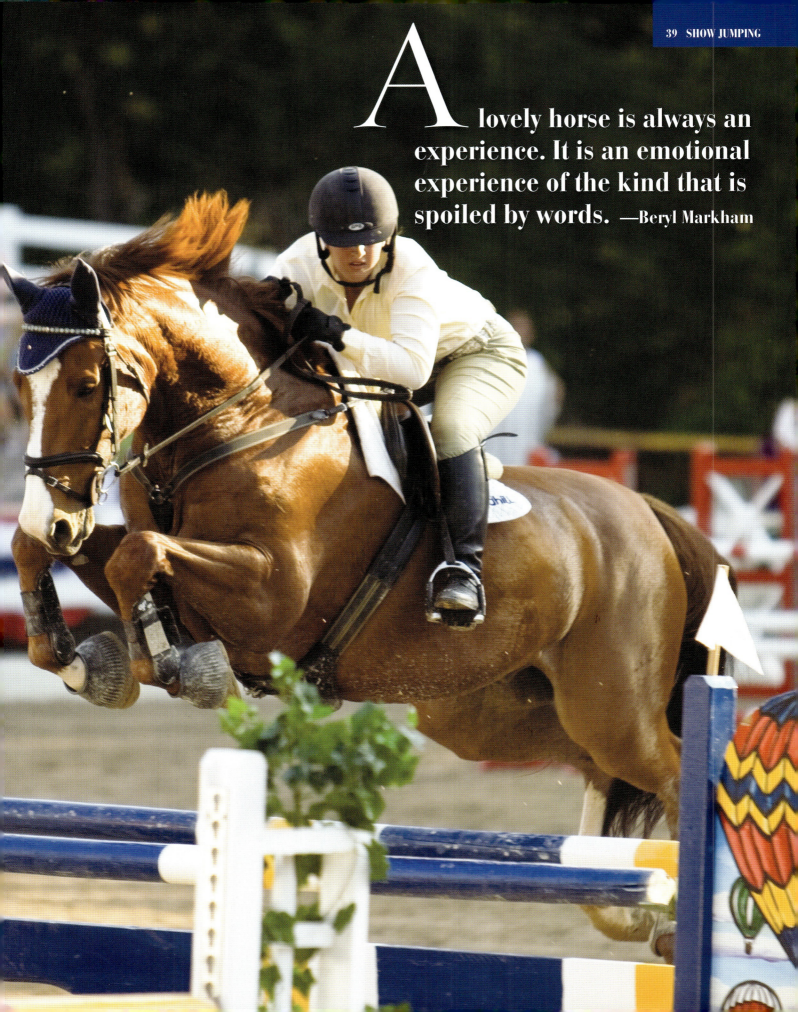

A lovely horse is always an experience. It is an emotional experience of the kind that is spoiled by words. —Beryl Markham

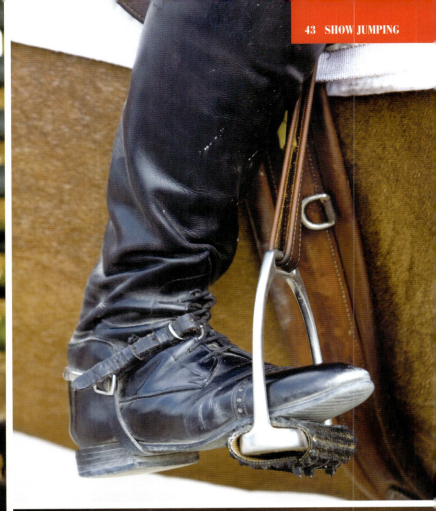

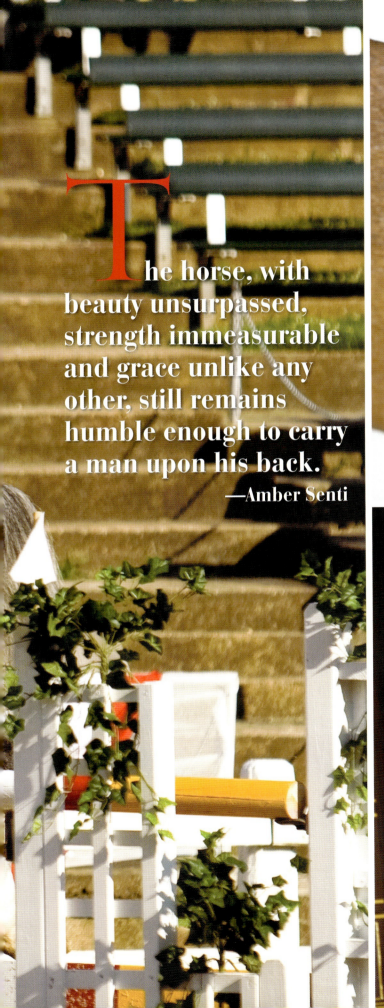

The horse, with beauty unsurpassed, strength immeasurable and grace unlike any other, still remains humble enough to carry a man upon his back.
—Amber Senti

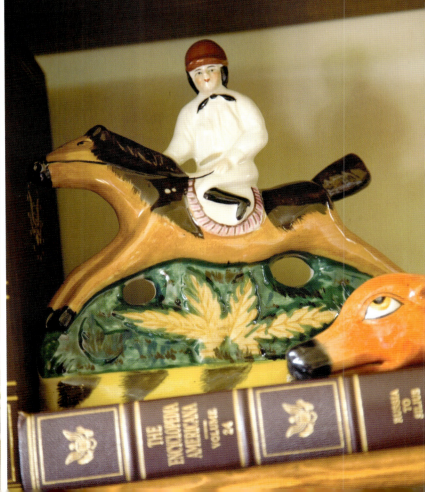

RACING

The stunning

cast-stone fireplace is the perfect focal point in this comfortable living room. Proudly displayed on Mike McGuire's mantel is a lovely oil painting of jockey and horse behind a bronze sculpture of mare and colt, paired with two beautiful red tole urns. Schotzie, Mike's beloved schnauzer, sits in her favorite chair.

Mike McGuire's charming home is full of equine art, Staffordshire, and race-horse treasures. When it came time to find a place to display his collection, Mike designed a comfortable, cozy retreat where he would be surrounded by his favorite things.

Often, what is displayed on the mantel defines the décor of the room. True to form, in order to create the perfect focal point for his room, Mike decided to place his favorite oil painting of a horse and jockey as the centerpiece of the lovely custom-designed cast-stone mantel. The room is elegant yet comfortable, with its plush chairs and one-of-a-kind needlepoint horse pillows. Both sides of the room display Mike's many horse treasures, a collection started by Charles Faudree, who gave Mike his first stirrup cup as a gift because of Mike's love of horses. That was the beginning of Mike's amazing collection of equestrian memorabilia.

In Britain around the 1600s, it was King Charles II who was responsible for raising English participation and interest in racing. Prior to that, racing had been practiced by the Romans, who had picked it up from the Greeks. King Charles II developed the sport in the town of Newmarket, Suffolk, where he was both organizer and competitor. He used his royal authority to arrange races and establish rules. Prior to these formalized races, racing had typically been a simple match between two horses to settle a bet between their owners. It was in 1634 that the first cup race was endowed. In those days the racehorses were all native-bred. In the north, there were Galloways, known for their speed. Ireland had Hobby horses. As the popularity evolved, horses began to be imported, initially from Italy and Spain

A horse gallops with his lungs, perseveres with his heart, and wins with his character. —Amber Senti

and then from North Africa, the Eastern Mediterranean, and Arabia. It was the mixing of the native-bred and the bloodlines from these imports that established the Thoroughbred as a breed in its own right. In the United States, the classic three-year-old races were instituted in the decade following the Civil War. First came the Belmont Stakes in New York in 1867, named for the leading owner and breeder August Belmont; next were the Preakness Stakes in 1873, running on the Pimlico course near Baltimore, Maryland; and then came the Kentucky Derby at Churchill Downs in 1875, in Louisville. The three together form the legendary Triple Crown program.

Bill Mullen's great room is elegant yet comfortable. An oil painting of a Scotsman hangs over the cast-stone fireplace made by local Tulsa artist Jim Kelly, and proudly oversees the living space. The country French side chairs, made by Masters Custom Woodcraft, are covered with wonderful Marquis fabric called "Gladiateur," so named because the horse pictured on

the fabric is the Gladiateur who won the English Triple Crown in 1865. A beautiful design choice in Bill's home is his antique pine coffee table with a horse bronze. Bookshelves provide an interesting way to display his beautiful antique horse plates, placed symmetrically alongside leather-bound books and Staffordshire figurines.

A replica of a Majolica umbrella holder of a pair of riding boots is the perfect place in an entry hall for gathering a collection of canes, walking sticks, and horse umbrellas. Along with the canes is an antique hand-painted chair depicting the 1832 Horse Racing winner, Collina, *facing, above left.*

A charming vignette of an antique chest and Victorian horned mirror is complemented by a bronze of a jockey and horse with brown-and-white horse plates, *facing, above right.* A gorgeous bronze of a winning jockey has been repurposed into a fun and practical lamp, *facing, below left.*

Totally money driven, this king of sports and the sport of kings has generated millions of dollars in prize money and wagers. Today, the United States holds the premier position on the world racing stage.

Mike McGuire of Tulsa, Oklahoma, has loved horses for years and owned a beloved American Quarter Horse named Mouse, whom he bought when Mouse was three months old. Mike saw this horse being born and knew there would always be a special place in his heart for it. Mouse's mom did not have enough milk, so Mike started bottle-feeding him. There was such a bond between Mike and Mouse that it kept them together for thirty-one years! Mouse would follow Mike around everywhere like a dog. Mouse was a great horse to the end, and they had many enjoyable hours and years together. Mike misses his dear friend Mouse.

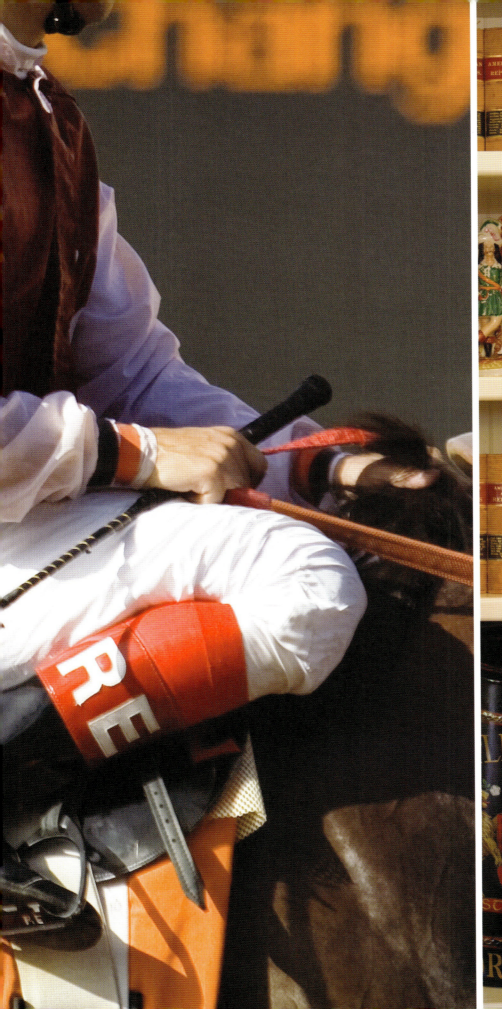

A beautiful design choice in Bill Mullen's home is his antique pine coffee table with a horse bronze and a nineteenth-century match striker he purchased in London. The "Gladiateur" fabric on the side chairs continues the theme and brings the room together, *left.* An antique lithograph of horse and jockey, circa 1851, is centered between a pair of silver French 1750s wine coolers that Annie Uechtritz inherited from her grandmother, *facing.*

POLO

A newly remodeled mud-
room helps to maintain
the family's polo boots,
mallets, and helmets,
while artfully exhibit-
ing the family's love and
enthusiasm for the sport,
facing, above left.

Polo is one of the oldest games

played on horseback, having originated
in China over two thousand years ago. It
is played with a ball and mallet, typically
with four players on each team. Since the
migration of polo from China to America
via India and Great Britain in the 1870s,
polo has become an international horse
sport that is represented all over the world.
Introduced in the United States in 1876 by
James Gordon Bennett, an Englishman
who brought horses to be trained for the
game, polo became popular in the States
in the 1920s and '30s during national and
international polo competitions. Now the
game is mainly played on the club level
under the U.S. Polo Association.

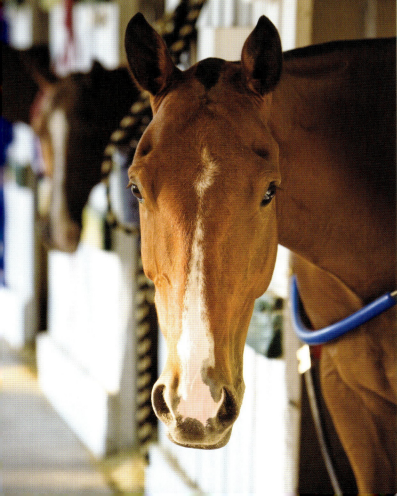

Annie and Bernie Uechtritz's light-filled colonial-style great room features beautiful dark wood floors and a pair of sofas, slip-covered in white and accented with fresh blue-and-white ticking pillows. Annie's antique pine farm table serves as a coffee table, displaying a fabulous polo bronze by Remington along with many of her horse books and home interior books.

BUNNY WILLIAMS AN AFFAIR WITH A HOUSE

LALANDE & TRILLARD   The New Eighteenth-Ce

ITALY

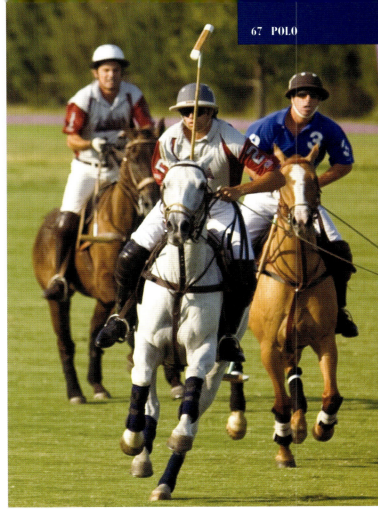

Centered between two white orchids in blue-and-white cache pots, the polo bronze takes center stage, *left.*

The horse and rider in this sport

are, as in all the disciplines in this book, a team. Relying on their strength, stamina and agility, the horses in the field antici-pate what their riders are going to ask of them. It is a beautiful dance, and these big-hearted horses will do whatever their riders ask. A great polo horse has to gal-lop flat out, stop in his own length, turn on a dime, turn at 180 degrees, and start off from a standstill and then go at top speed in any direction, all with a mallet swinging around his body and polo balls being hit toward him. The game is played in chuk-kas of seven and a half minutes each. There can be four, six, seven, or eight chukkas—today there are usually four or six; there are three minutes between chukkas and a five-minute break at halftime. Every time a goal is scored the teams change ends, so the stamina and endurance of the polo horse is crucial. Each player usually has more than one horse per match.

Whether you regard the horse with awe or love it is impossible to escape the sheer power of his presence.   —Mary Wanless

Annie's dining room is impressive with its pair of ten-foot tables reclaimed from a French boys' school. The table is surrounded by lovely French chairs and a long country-style bench, which help to create flexible seating for a family meal. An antique hutch provides beautiful and practical storage space, while an exquisite crystal chandelier lights the room.

Bernie and Annie Uechtritz grew up riding horses, he in Papua New Guinea and Australia, and she in Texas. While Annie rode western, Bernie spent most of his time on horseback playing

POLO AND POLOCROSSE

—an Australian sport that Bernie has been introducing and promoting in America since 1989. Now that they have children, Bernie and Annie are passing their love of horses and polo on to the next generation, teaching their children the love of a horse.

In trying to make their dreams reality, Annie and Bernie

and their four children found property in Dallas that was full of potential. The property included a main house, a guest house, and a barn, and would allow them room for their polo horses and to create the home they'd always wanted. Their love and respect for tradition inspired them to re-create a beautiful old Southern Colonial home from a 1960s wood-frame ranch house. Annie's thoughtfulness and attention to detail was so transformative that when I asked her about her lovely historic home, she was proud to tell me it was only forty-eight years old. Good job, Annie!

Bill Mullen gets ready for a brunch using his
Ralph Lauren polo dishes and mugs. His dining
table centerpiece is sophisticated and beautiful;
a charmingly rustic basket full of flowers
surrounding an antique Staffordshire figurine
provides a fresh take on a classic piece. Floral
arrangement by Toni's Flowers and Gifts, Tulsa.

HORSES & CHILDREN

Olivia Uechtritz and her pony, Blackie, have their very own playhouse. The building is a tiny version of the Uechtritzes' main house in Dallas, *left*. In this beautiful princess-inspired crib in Ellie's bedroom, the gorgeous cascading ruffles create functional shade for napping while creating a dreamy fairy tale space that any girl would be proud to call her own, *facing, below right*.

We were all kids once, and for most of us that was when our love of horses first began to grow. Kids share a special bond with their first horse; mine was Prince and he was my very best friend. I still remember and miss him, even now.

These future equestrian stars bring a smile to every spectator's face. The children are so excited for their very first blue ribbon experience. The lead line class at the Germantown Charity Horse Show in Tennessee was another fun way for the very youngest equestrians to be included.

Alexandra Burt's Breyer horse collection is quite impressive, *facing*. This little girl, happy and smiling in her pink riding helmet and John Deere T-shirt, competes in the Lead Line event in Germantown, Tennessee. In lead line competitions, children are led around the ring on their horses with a parent or guardian firmly in control of the lead. *right.*

Many horse shows have lead line and stick horse

classes for children. The lead line is a class in which the horses are led by a lead line, or kind of leash, with the children mounted on the horse's back. It's a simple way for children to be included in the horse show and is fun for everyone. This particular class was in Germantown, Tennessee, and every child won a blue ribbon.

The bond between kids and their horses translates into magical rooms filled with stuffed horses, collections of Breyer model horses, and antique rocking horses. Some of the best aspects of these kids' rooms prove that old traditions are still alive. In an age of video games and cell phones, *Black Beauty* and *My Friend Flicka* can still be found on bookshelves.

Large sliding glass doors lead to the backyard and are framed by gauzy hangings, creating a bright and airy bedroom. Splashes of black and bright pink give the room both definition and pizzazz.

When I walked into LuAnn Luekemeyer's granddaughter's room, I thought, "Ellie is the luckiest grandbaby in the world!" I loved it—I would love to live in it myself, but no crib necessary! The modern black-and-white of the décor was appealing, but more than that, splashes of fuchsia and the horses, of course, made the room pop with color and attitude. It is a beautiful room with a perfect blend of modern design and a child's love of horses.

Horses and children, I often think, have a lot of the good sense there is in the world. —Josephine Demott Robison

When LuAnn designed the room, she knew she wanted one room that would continue to grow with Ellie throughout her childhood, into her teen years, and beyond. Ellie's mother, Mary Brit, had loved horses as a child, so it was important to LuAnn to incorporate that love into the design. The white backdrop of the walls and the leather furniture, perfect for the young horse-lover now, create a canvas that will allow her to add her own flair for years to come.

Olivia Uechtritz loves to draw her horse, Blackie. When she drew this picture of herself on Blackie, her mother had it gorgeously framed and hung in her dressing area instead of on the refrigerator. This is a wonderful way to appreciate children's art and incorporate it into the design of a room, *left*. A well-loved antique rocking horse is the highlight of the charming nursery in Jan Barsted's home, *facing*.

There are
friends and **faces**
that may be forgotten,
but there are **horses**
that never will be.

—Andy Adams

WORKING HORSES

Chico Bond, a cowboy and horse trainer

whose training style I will forever respect, is an intriguing individual. Chico calls himself a "natural horseman." His training style is more resistance free, common sense, pressure and release, and training through consistency. Chico says, "I form a partnership with the horses I start. I present them with a method they can understand. Horses don't like conflict, they don't have egos, they are not trying to impress anyone. They just want to get along." The cowboy tradition *does* live on.

W

hat better way to feel a part of all earth and sky.
That whirling over hill and dale on hoofs that seem to fly.

—Laura Chester,
from "Heartbeat for Horses"

In a book about horses, it would be a mistake not to include the American tradition of working horses, cowboys,
and cattle drives. Being a cowboy is not just what was por-
trayed on *Bonanza* and *The Rifleman*; it's a way of life. I

completely and utterly get the cowboy life: the breathtak-
ing vistas of Texas countryside, combined with the sunset
backlighting trees and lowing cows transported me back
a hundred and fifty years to a time when Texas was new

and cowboy country wasn't just a way of life but was *the* way of life.

The cowboy life was on horseback taking care of cattle. Cattle drives were needed to gather the cattle for branding and to get the cattle from the ranches to market or to other land for grazing. Team roping developed back on the ranches when cowboys needed to capture and handle full-grown cattle and steers for branding or "doctoring."

This elegant

western-style dining room makes dining enjoyable with its antique English dining chairs and primitive table. A hanging chandelier of antlers and a cowboy-themed oil painting reinforce the western décor.

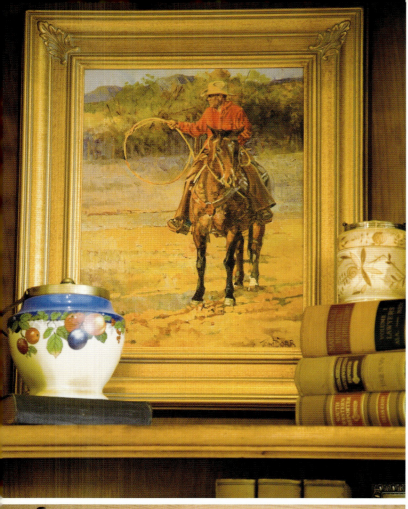

The Abernathys' lovely great room features a gorgeous brick fireplace with a lovely pastoral oil painting flanked by green vases on the mantel. Two lovely chairs and an ottoman complete the room and are covered in "Tissu Fleuri" fabric by Schumacher, *facing*.

From the bunkhouse to the big house, it doesn't have to be all chaps and cowboy hats, which is exemplified by Connie and Mike Abernathy's wonderful country estate. Jennifer Spak of V&S Designs designed the room as a study of rustic refinement, bringing together primitive pine cabinetry and rough-hewn stone with elegant furniture and sumptuous fabrics. Plush French bergère chairs, a brilliantly colored antique Mahal rug, and a limestone fireplace create a comfortable and inviting setting to display the couple's collection of cowboy-themed art.

The Albernathys'
bright and airy bedroom—with
its Victorian wrought-iron
bedstead, candle sconces, coffered
ceilings with architectural detail,
and oil painting of a cattle drive—
continues to evoke a rustic feel. To
provide a bit of contrast, designer
Jennifer Spak chose imported
English linens in muted tones to
bring a touch of sophistication. The
result is a soothing, charmingly
rustic refuge from the hustle and
bustle of the world.

That cowboy tradition carries through

to western design. Western design is about rustic simplicity, relaxing spaces, and soothing earthy palettes. In her reinterpretation of a barn bunkhouse, Mimi Rogers melds a touch of sensible practicality with a soothing, simple atmosphere to create a beautiful and relaxing space out of what was once a tack room. Cement floors and earth-toned linens make this a practical and functional room, especially when you are coming in for a bit of a rest after a dusty trail ride. Original doors and reclaimed wood cabinetry provide a bit of rustic contrast to the soothing robins' egg blue of the walls and evoke a certain western charm. Practical hooks on the doors provide a place to stow chaps and cowboy hats for quick and easy use.

This room was created in Mimi's barn to allow her guests closer access to the horses. Decorated in soothing earth tones, it creates a serene oasis for any traveler—especially cowboys. You'd never know this was once a tack room!

LEISURE
TIME

Priscilla Darling and her horse, Top Gun's Good Girl, take a refreshing drink from the creek on her afternoon trail ride, *left*. Lynn Walsh spends time with Beautiful Parker, the warmblood, and her golden retriever, Chester, *facing*.

People have been riding horses

for pleasure for centuries upon centuries. Not only are we able to explore our bonds with our horses through pleasure riding, but we are able to commune with nature and get some exercise too! A leisurely afternoon ride through the meadows provides ample opportunity to catch up with an old friend or bond with your four-legged companion. A horse can be a loyal comrade in the competition ring or on the trail.

My favorite time has always been when I go to the barn and groom my horse—it's a time of solitude and quiet, and it takes me back to memories of childhood trail rides with Prince.

Landon Darling takes her friend Catherine Benton on a fun and memorable ride on her gentle bay, *left*. This dining room is the epitome of country sophistication. The table is a reclaimed door that has been given a new life in this home and is the perfect match for the arched windows that artfully display a collection of dishware and horseshoes, *facing*.

Decorating with painted horseshoes guarantees my guests good luck. Pictured in my kitchen sitting area *(shown on page 100)* are good luck wishes illustrated in a tramp art-framed good luck horseshoe, along with transferware, framed photos of my family—Sister, and Sadie, Bailey and me—on my 1940s barkcloth-skirted table.

This new kitchen was designed in keeping this 1880s Texas farmhouse's original structure, all the way down to the exposed beams and lap-and-gap boards from the original walls, repurposed as crown molding. The design continues with the open shelving, similar to the way it would have been in the 1880s.

Originally two separate rooms, the kitchen is now one great open space. In keeping with the

idea of a country kitchen, open cabinetry creates an eclectic and homey feel. A kitchen still needs to be functional, though, so updates were made to install stainless steel appliances and modern light fixtures.

True to the equine theme in every room in this country home, a copper weather vane with beautiful patina sits proudly on a Texas primitive dining table.

Pillows in a Charles Faudree equestrian toile fabric for Vervain accent a charming 1880s carriage house. Antique horn beakers are part of the side table vignette. They were carried by riders on a hunt and would be used for a toast once the quarry had been captured. Several of the beakers are embellished with silver monogrammed crests; one holds a collection of porcupine quills.

W

hat a joy. To sit on his back like a throne, to touch heaven while still on earth, remain together for years, companions in journeys and dreams!

—Juan Llamas

Lynn and Susan have a relaxing leisure ride around the lake, *left*. Robert Smith enjoys the wind in his hair and the speed underneath him as he rides freely, *above*. In this bedroom, bright and cheerful bedding provides a lovely setting for a Donna Howell Sickles sketch of a galloping horse. A charming bedside table completes the room with a glass lamp, a ceramic pitcher of Belinda's Dream roses, and a pretty and colorful horse plate, *facing*.

GARDENS

The water feature at the Wheats' home in Texas provides the best seat in the house for relaxing while listening to the sounds of water falling from hammered copper bowls. A reflecting pool's limestone-and-cast-cement structure adds elegance to this garden view, *facing.* Diane Smith's Charleston-style front porch welcomes her guests, *previous overleaf.*

Horses belong in nature, and what better way for them to be incorporated into décor than in outdoor rooms, gardens, and exteriors. Stone and metal sculptures that peek out of beautifully planted cottage-style gardens add elegance and style to an otherwise simple landscape. Outdoor sitting areas, casual or elegant, benefit from classic equestrian statuary and plaques that garden visitors can enjoy while sipping their morning coffee or relaxing in the afternoon shade.

One of my favorite gardens is Bill Mullen's outdoor patio entertaining area. The gorgeous pergola creates a shaded, cool, and comfortable area to sit and enjoy the beautifully landscaped gardens of his Tulsa home. His collections are on display there as well, with a jockey sculpture providing a whimsical touch of light during evening entertaining.

In my own country cottage-style

gardens, winding beds of native flowers and shrubs are accented by stone sculptures and copper weather vanes. These horses create a focal point, a way to draw the eye through the gardens. One of my favorite pieces is a stone sculpture of a horse head that once belonged to my father. It sits in my garden now in one of my favorite spots, and every time it catches my eye, it reminds me of him, *above*.

God forbid that I should go to any heaven in which there are no horses!   —R. B. Cunningham

Diane Smith's lovely Charleston-style garden in Texas welcomes her guests, complete with rocking chairs, chaise lounges, and a wonderful etched-and-stained checked concrete patio that she stained herself.

Kissed by sunlight, embraced by open fields.
The horse is the center of all beautiful things.   —Walt Morey

While visiting horse shows in Kentucky, I saw some of the most amazing iconic horse farms in the country. Vast stretches of gorgeous Kentucky blue grass and miles of white fences made for stunning roadside views, while the barns themselves were classic and elegant—literally palaces for horses!

I love a beautiful horse barn and facility. I can appreciate the pride and hard work their upkeep requires. There's nothing prettier than a barn with awe-inspiring architecture and what it represents: the horse's home and lifestyle. I love the traditional building, the turrets, the hitching posts. I love the smell of the hay and the horses. I love the sound of their neighing. I love to pet their muzzles. These things make me feel like I've come home.

ANTIQUES

The silver trophies and loving cups

presented to winning horses and riders are favorite items among collectors of equestrian memorabilia. Loving cups are prized not only for their beauty but for their practicality as well. I often see them used in homes as vases for flower arrangements, both in groups and as accent pieces. These cups are becoming increasingly difficult to find at a bargain, so if you come across one, snatch it up!

My good friend Betty Danielson is an avid collector. She's been browsing the flea markets for nearly fifty years, and her collections have evolved and changed as much as she has. Everywhere you look in her home there is an interesting new find. One of her favorite things to collect is horse memorabilia, especially vintage good-luck-themed items.

A hunt scene atop the antique faux tortoiseshell cigarette case graces the middle of an arrangement of real tortoiseshell boxes, *below left.* A stately English portrait defines this dining room. It is surrounded by a beautiful collection of majolica plates along with transferware and a grouping of Staffordshire horse and rider figurines, *facing.*

Staffordshire pottery refers not to any one

manufacturer or style but instead to any pottery or ceramics that come from an area called the Potteries in Staffordshire County, England, dating back to the late 1600s. More than three dozen manufacturers can fall under the Staffordshire umbrella, and some of the better-known potteries include Spode, Minton, Royal Doulton, and Wedgwood. Equestrian figurines are some of the most collectible of the Staffordshire porcelain. As a collection, equestrian figures can create a beautiful traditional feel in any room. A fresh take on the Staffordshire figurine has them repurposed into lamps or used as showpieces in floral arrangements, but they are also displayed as valuable works of art in their own right.

Bill Mullen had his favorite antique Staffordshire made into a charming lamp complete with a custom-made paisley lamp shade. Completing the vignette are a modern pair of ceramic riding boots for holding reading glasses and a miniature racing print, *facing*.

I like to learn something new every day,

and when I visited Mike McGuire's home in Tulsa, I learned about stirrup cups. I noticed in Mike's great room that there was a collection of hollow Staffordshire fox heads. When I asked about them and what they were used for, Mike explained that they were used to celebrate a successful hunt. The cups were placed in the boot of a hunter, and once the fox was finally caught, the cups were pulled out and a toast was poured to celebrate the completion of the hunt.

Antiquing is a great way to gather new collections or to complete existing ones. Antiques fairs and flea markets often provide amazing selections of horse accoutrements that are perfect for home décor: games, rugs, and tins, as well as tableware, prints, and decorative Staffordshire figurines.

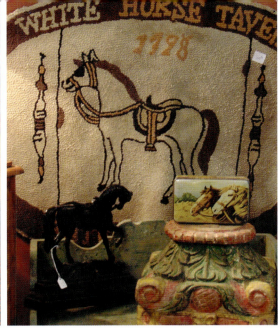

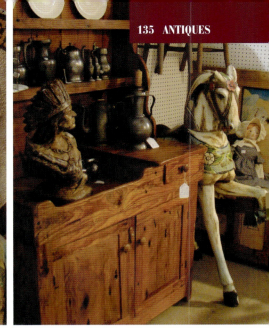

The love of a horse truly influences

how we decorate our homes, what we collect, what we wear, and how we spend our leisure time. Equine treasures are everywhere to be found. You might come upon some unexpected ones similar to those shown here, as you sort through toy chests, attics, and boxes saved from childhood.

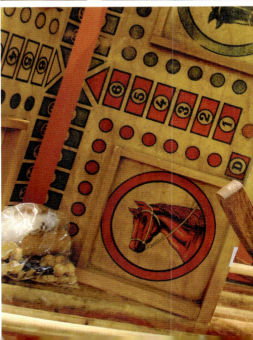

DRESSAGE

Though classic in training, dressage is another form of horseback riding that embodies the horse and rider as a team. Spectators of this event can attest that it is as if a beautiful dance were being performed. The patience and obedience of the horse is so evident in dressage. The dressage horse has such a big heart that it will do anything for its rider. The challenge of the sport itself, coupled with the concentration and time needed to train a dressage horse, has resulted in a way of life in which people find great pleasure, great interest, and a relaxing pastime. Each rider and horse shows passion and devotion to their sport.

Dressage principles of the modern age demand that the horse should be active and free but still display power and speed. There can be only a light contact on the reins, and there should be little visible effort to control the horse. The horse must be calm, supple, submissive, and willing to adjust its paces without resistance. The horse should also remain perfectly straight from head to tail, and all gaits should be in perfect regularity of rhythm.

Sometimes he trots as if told the steps,
with gentle majesty on modest pride.
—William Shakespeare

Dressage is an elegant dance of true harmony

between horse and rider. The Greeks established forms of what would become dressage as far back as the fourth or fifth centuries BC, and it is known today as the most classical form of horseback riding. The Greeks' training of their horses in this tradition was seen as artistic and a pleasurable accomplishment as well as a means of improving the performance of their cavalry. The term *dressage* didn't come to be until the early eighteenth century. It is derived from the French verb *dresser*, which means "to train, to straighten out, or to adjust."

Primarily used by the military and learned through training at cavalry schools, dressage training was thought to be a gentlemanly accomplishment by the wealthy in royal courts and similar centers of culture. These courtiers quickly spread interest in dressage training, and dressage soon expanded into a competitive sport. The first dressage competition of the Olympics was ridden during the Stockholm Games of 1912.

Mimi Rogers' kitchen, with its exposed beam ceilings and leather accessories, is reminiscent of a stable, while the stainless steel appliances and cool lines of the backsplash and white glass-fronted cabinetry create a modern look that appeals to even a traditional aesthetic. A gorgeous carved

jade horse head adds a bit of color to the room and accents the green tile of the backsplash. This kitchen melds modern and traditional by adopting clean lines of green granite countertops and stainless steel as well as traditional exposed beams and black leather chairs.

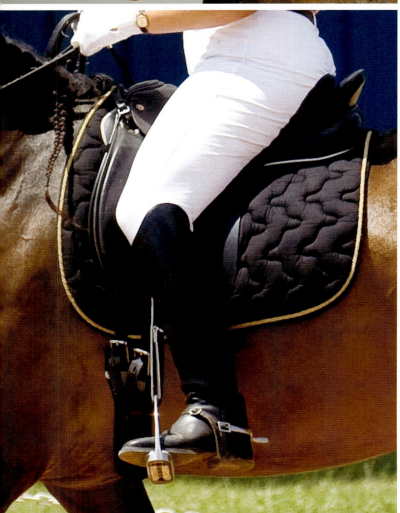

The Wheats' home in Texas is an example of

modern design, incorporating clean lines, calming colors, and the resonance of eclectic furnishings to create a harmonious melding of tradition and modernity. Much like dressage, this interior space is all about lines. In creating this design, Jennifer Spak began with the sleek lines of the white leather side chairs, and the minimalist modern design that Laura Wheat wanted evolved from there. Geometric designs on the linens draw the eye to the bed immediately, where a riot of color and shapes makes a commanding statement. A lovely bronze of a mare and her colt provides one of very few curved lines in the room and is a beautiful addition to the side table.

"Pomegranate
and Roses"
by Harold Kraus is proudly
displayed above a modern
settee covered in a lovely
bold-striped Ralph Lauren
fabric.

DRIVING

When I purchased my current
home in 2004, it was a serious fixer-upper.
I have never backed down
from a challenge, though, and one of the selling
features of the property was a

CARRIAGE
HOUSE

built in the 1880s, complete with
two intact antique carriages. It took a lot of work
to renovate the carriage house,
but the finished result—with its gorgeous wood
floors, refinished and waxed original
pine walls, interesting architectural details, and
big comfy bed draped with
equestrian linens—has made it one of my favorite guest cottages at my bed and breakfast.

Driving is still an intensely competitive, major international horse sport. It can be seen locally in regional horse shows, as well as in major competitions such as the World Equestrian Games. This discipline requires great skill and can prove challenging due to the inherent remove of rider from horse. Driving evokes a feeling of the Old West, Regency balls, and ancient fighting chariots—it's a sport almost as old as history itself.

This high-stepping Hackney pony shows his stuff and his blue in this harness class at the Lexington Junior League Horse Show in Lexington, Kentucky.

Jennifer's kitchen puts her love of blue and white on display. A French-style milk-painted table with four chairs, newly recovered with blue crewel fabric, provide the perfect space for entertaining. The white marble countertops and pale blue bead board ceiling make the kitchen bright and inviting.

My friend Jennifer Spak's kitchen in McKinney, Texas, is a wonderful interpretation of a blue-and-white country kitchen. Jennifer, interior designer and owner of V&S Designs, says she has been collecting china and dinnerware with her mother and sister for years and that any shade of blue will

work in her kitchen. Much of the blue-and-white china she has collected depicts scenes of driving or horses and carriages.

Images that evoke driving can tastefully dress up your walls and decorate your tabletops. A framed carriage-inspired scarf, gingham fabric of the table skirt, a stack of books, and two wooden inlaid boxes complete this vignette. *facing*. This gorgeous Saddlebred won this harness class at the Junior League Horse Show in Lexington, Kentucky. *right*.

The epitome of

a horse tradition, driving teams have been a part of the history of the world almost as long as the horse itself, from Roman chariots to English carriages to covered wagons. Apart from competition, this age-old mode of transportation seems to now be limited mostly to the Amish, parades, and romantic rides through city parks and historical districts.

A repurposed spirit barrel made into a lamp with a carriage scene proudly sits in Lynn Walsh's den, *left*. An antique china dish on display boasts a horse and wagon from yesteryear, *below left*.

A horse is a beautiful animal, but perhaps most remarkable because it moves as though it always hears music.

—Mark Helprin

SADDLEBRED

The elegant Saddlebred was developed in

Kentucky by plantation owners of the nineteenth century, who needed a smooth-gaited horse to ride and oversee their land for hours and hours. Saddlebreds were also excellent for pulling a harness for a smooth Sunday afternoon drive. The foundation sire was a Thoroughbred called Denmark, foaled in 1839. The breed also contains elements of the Morgan, a breed known for its great physical strength. In earlier times, Saddlebred horses were predominantly chestnut, bay, or black, but today they may also be paint, gray, and palomino.

Today the Saddlebred breed is bred for the show ring, where there are three types of competition: in harness, three-gaited, and five-gaited classes. The gaits represented are walk, trot, canter, and slow gait and rack, respectively. The showy five-gaited Saddlebred is the aristocrat of the breed and best demonstrates elegance and speed with its high-stepping action and beautiful animated walk. The showy appearance of a Saddlebred is accentuated by high head and tail carriage and a high-stepping action, where the knees come above the horse's chest. In the show ring, the riders demonstrate the traditions of long ago by continuing to wear traditional suits or tuxedoes and top hats. With riders in their show attire, the horses groomed to perfection, and the roar of the crowd, a Saddlebred horse show, to me, is the most exciting of all!

Horses are fiercely loyal and committed. They give us tremendous gifts, if we allow ourselves to be open to them.

—Kate Soliste-Mattelon

I love to use old hitching post heads as towel racks and loving cups as flower vases, utensil holders, pen receptacles, a place to put hairbrushes, or anything that strikes my fancy. One particular idea is putting pantry, closet, and bathroom doors on barn hardware tracks. They are like pocket doors but without the fuss of heavy construction. It's amazing how much space you can save when you don't need to allow for a door clearance!

My advice to you in shopping for horse décor is to keep your eyes open at all times. You never know what you'll find. Eight years ago I was in Round Top, Texas, during their biannual antique show. As I was walking amongst the rows and rows of vendors' tents, some antique French equestrian toile drapes caught my eye. They were complete with the drapery hardware in them and matched my living room exactly! I quickly asked how much they cost, and the man said that he didn't know because they were his wife's and that she'd just gone to lunch. I offered him a low amount, knowing he would say no or that we'd have to wait for his wife, but instead he said okay! I shopped the rest of the day, and in three different situations, I was offered over four times what I paid for them.

I had to be creative and lengthen the drapes, so I bought complementary fabric to make a valance and added the same fabric on the bottom of the curtains so they would work in my living room. These equestrian toile drapes were a great purchase—so classic and versatile that I have moved homes with them three times, and they are still in my living room today.

A horse is a thing of beauty . . . none will tire of looking at him as long as he displays

I have been collecting horse memorabilia

with my dear friend Cindy Kolmeier for many years, and we both enjoy the thrills of the flea markets and antique malls.

Cindy's twenty years of showing and breeding Saddlebreds has greatly influenced her home-decorating style. Loving cups and silver bowls are wonderful additions when bought at stores, but when you actually win them they mean so much more. Her home is also filled with equestrian art pieces. For example, a pair of cement horse head statues is used as the centerpiece on her dining room table, and she has an antique brass weather vane in her breakfast room.

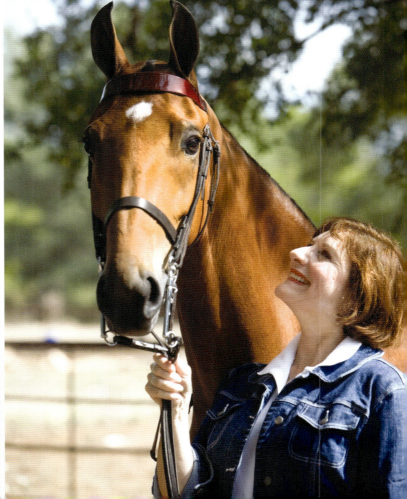

Another of my favorite pieces hangs in my foyer. In 1992, years after my horse Johnny G had died, I commissioned Donna Howell Sickles, my favorite artist, to do a portrait of Johnny G and me together. Having a portrait of us hanging in my home allows me to see and remember him every day.

My Saddlebred experience has had a great influence on my own home décor. Throughout my home, I proudly display my collections of loving cups and silver trophies, horn cups used for toasting before a hunt, equestrian fabrics, drawings and paintings of horses, and ceramics—just to name a few. I incorporate horses into every aspect of my interior design, from a copper horse weather vane centerpiece to horse plates on the wall. I particularly appreciate when items can be repurposed or used in an innovative way to create function.

Embrace your passions and let them be seen—decorate with them, display them. Your favorite things, whatever they may be, are what will make a house your home.

ACKNOWLEDGMENTS

I want to sincerely thank all the wonderful people and horses who helped me make my vision come true.

First, I need to thank all the homeowners, including Jennifer Spak; Lynn Walsh; Bill Mullen; Mike McGuire; Betty Danielson; Cindy Kolmeier; Susan Pelletier; Annie, Olivia, and Bernie Uechtritz; Laura Wheat; Connie Abernathy; LuAnn Lueckemeyer; Paula, Catherine, and Bill Benton; Priscilla and Landon Darling; Jan Barstad; Diane Smith; Mimi Rogers; Alexandra Burt; and Joan Godwin.

Special thanks to my dear friend Nancy Ingram for her friendship and support, and also for her help with the photo styling at Bill Mullen's and Mike McGuire's homes.

Thanks also to my good friend Cindy Kolmeier for her friendship and unending support throughout this process, and for always being there for me.

Thank you to my good friend Charles Faudree for his support and encouragement, and for dressing my carriage house with one of his beautiful toiles from his new line of fabrics, the Charles Faudree Collection for Vervain.

I would also like to thank my friend Jennifer Spak of V&S Designs in McKinney, Texas, who understood my concept and not only helped me find locations but helped style the shots and was a wonderful "flower lady." Thanks also to Gina Tomelleri Galichia of Country Garden Antiques in Dallas, Texas, for her help in finding and photo styling the Uechtritz home. Thanks are also due to Bill Benton and all the team-roping cowboys and the cattle drive cowboys; Chico Bond; Fran Dearing, the great dressage riders, and the horses of Windy Knoll Farm; Bernie Uechtritz and the other polo players of the North Texas Polo Club; the Houston Polo Club; the fabulous show jumpers, driving classes, and children at the Germantown Charity Horse Show in Germantown, Tennessee; the horses, riders, children, and driving classes at the Junior League Charity Horse Show in Lexington, Kentucky; the riders and horses at the Country Heir Horse Show at the Horse Park in Lexington, Kentucky; the horses and jockeys at Lone Star Park in Grand Prairie, Texas; Karen Dawkins at Smitten in McKinney, Texas; Terry Rogers at Chase Hall Antiques, McKinney, Texas; and Vicki Woods at Home-pieces in McKinney, Texas.

I also want to give a big thank-you to my friend Charlotte Whatley for helping me pull this all together through her excellent editing, organizational, and computer skills, and for never forgetting to bring me breakfast.

Finally, I have to thank my babies, Sister, Bailey, and Sadie. To Sister and Bailey for always being here for me unconditionally, for being the best travelers, for keeping me company, and for patiently waiting while I was shooting. And to Sadie, thanks for always being with me; the three of us miss you dearly.

RESOURCES

CALIFORNIA
Villa Melrose
6061 W. 3rd Street
Los Angeles, CA 90036
323.934.8130

Lyman Drake
2901 S. Harbor Boulevard
Santa Ana, CA 92704
714.979.2811

Kathleen Stewart
338 N. La Brea Avenue
Los Angeles, CA 90036
323.931.6676

FLORIDA
Wellington & Company
Wellington, FL 33414
561.358.1164
wellingtonandco@bellsouth.net

KENTUCKY
The American Saddlebred Museum Gift Shop
4083 Iron Works Parkway
Lexington, KY 40511
859.255.4909

Sharing Horse Antiques & Gifts
Farmers, KY 40319
606.784.3806

Racing and Riding Collectibles
PO Box 1272
Versailles, KY 40383
859.351.6075

NEW HAMPSHIRE
Equine Antiques & Collectibles
208 Snow Road
Effingham, NH 03882
603.539.7739
oldhorsestuff@ttlc.net

NEW YORK
Chisholm Gallery, LLC
3 Factory Lane
Pine Plains, NY 12567
518.398.1246

George N. Antiques
67 E. 79th Street
New York City, NY 10022
212.223.9007

Kings Antiques
57 E. 11th Street
New York City, NY 10003
212.253.6000

NORTH CAROLINA
Thoroughbred Racing Memorabilia
311 Knollwood Drive
Hampstead, NC 28443

PENNSYLVANIA
Fox, Horse & Hound, Ltd.
P.O. Box 516
Kimberton, PA 19442
610.873.7909

OKLAHOMA
Antique Warehouse
Dale Gilman
2406 E. 12th Street
Tulsa, OK 74104
918.592.2900

Charles Faudree
1345 E. 15th Street
Tulsa, OK 74120
918.747.9706
www.charlesfaudree.com

Cisar Holt Inc.
1607 E. 15th Street
Tulsa, OK 74120
918.582.3080

Kelly's Antiques
210 W. Keetoowah Street
Tahlequah, OK 74461
918.456.0059

Polo Lodge Antiques
8250 E. 41st Street
Tulsa, OK 74145
918.622.3227

S. R. Hughes
3410 S. Peoria, Suite 100
Tulsa, OK 74105
918.742.5515
www.srhughes.com

T. A. Lorton
1345 E. 15th Street
Tulsa, OK 74120
918.743.1600
www.talorton.com

Toni's Flowers & Gifts
3549 S. Harvard Ave.
Tulsa, OK 74135
918.742.9027
1.800.526.9935
www.tonisflowersgifts.com

Windsor Market
6808 S. Memorial Drive, Suite 300
Tulsa, OK 74133
918.254.9766
www.windsormarket.com

TEXAS

Canterbury Antiques
2923-A N. Henderson Avenue
Dallas, TX 75206
214.821.5265

Chase Hall Antiques
Terry Rogers
205 E. Virginia
McKinney, TX 75069
972.548.1344

Country Garden Antiques
147 Parkhouse Street
Dallas, TX 75207
214.741.9331

The Gathering
955 Slocum Street
Dallas, TX 75207
214.741.4888
www.thegatheringantiques.com

Home Pieces
Vicki Woods
203 E. Virginia
McKinney, TX 75069
972.542.6191

HorsesandHomesOnline.com
Jenifer Jordan Photographer
horsesandhome@aol.com
jjordanphoto@aol.com
214.244.8614

Jenifer Jordan Photography
jjordanphoto@aol.com
www.horsesandhomes.com
214.244.8614

Legacy Antiques
1406 Slocum Street
Dallas, TX 75207
214.748.4606
www.legacyantiques.com

Legacy Trading Co.
3699 McKinney Avenue
Dallas, TX 75204
214.953.2222

Lots of Furniture
910 N. Industrial Boulevard
Dallas, TX 75207
214.761.1575
www.lotsoffurniture.com

The Mews
1708 Market Center Boulevard
Dallas, TX 75207
214.748.9070
www.themews.net

Nest Linens, Inc.
469.322.4367
info@nestlinens.com
www.nestlinens.com

The Old Grey Mare
16012 Old Coach Road
Magnolia, TX 77355
281.356.6991

Smitten
Karen Dawkins
118 E. Louisiana
McKinney, TX 75069
972.529.6994

Uncommon Market
2701 Fairmont Street
Dallas, TX 75201
214.871.2775
www.uncommonmarketinc.com

Uncommon Objects
1512 S. Congress Avenue
Austin, TX 78704
512.442.4000
www.uncommonobjects.com

V&S Designs
Jennifer Spak
P.O. Box 2798
McKinney, TX 75070
VandSDesigns@tx.rr.com

The Whimsey Shoppe
1444 Oak Lawn Avenue
Dallas, TX 75207
214.745.1800
www.thewhimseyshoppe.com

FLEA MARKETS AND ANTIQUE FAIRS
Round Top Antique Fair
475 N. Highway 237
Round Top, TX 78954
512.237.4747
www.roundtoptexasantiques.com

Round Top Art Fair and Creative Market
1235 N. Highway 237
Round Top, TX 78954
www.roundtopfolkartfair.com

Tulsa Flea Market
Tulsa Fairground
4145 E. 21st Street
Tulsa, OK 74114
918.744.1113